Feeling All My Worry

Kim T. S.

Kimi's worries, big and small,
Could build a tower ten feet tall!
She worries she can't get things right;

She's anxious
through a stormy night.

Let's
remember
that we're
safe.

She doesn't think it's very cool
To swim and frolic in the pool.

She frets about what friends might think,
And panics that the boat might sink!

"What if nightmares come tonight?
Will I ever sleep alright?"
Her heart beats fast; she starts to sweat.
There must be trouble brewing yet!

Rawr!!

Hush now, darling,
Please don't fear,
These feelings that you hold so near.
Worry helps you to reflect,
About the things you must protect.

Worry helps you
find ways to
protect what
matters to you.
But too much of it
can be harmful.

Feel your feelings, let them show.
Talk about them, let them go.
Close your eyes and breathe in deep;
Blow out worries that you keep.

I'll use calming
breaths to blow
out my worries!
It's okay
to cry.

The worries leave you as you blow;
Breathe out and watch the bubble grow.

Now wave your hand and say goodbye,
As they float up into the sky.

Once you're calm, and find release,
You must ACT to keep your peace.
Don't you worry, please take note:
<u>Action</u> is the antidote!

An antidote is a cure. It may sound easy, but taking action can be the hardest part! It's okay to ask for help!

Instead of
worrying,
I can do
something
about it!

Are you stressed about a test?
Just study hard and do your best.

Storms may come, but don't be scared—
You'll plan ahead and be prepared!

Practice and learn how to swim,
So you can jump in on a whim!

Wear a life vest on the boat,
So you'll be safe and stay afloat!

To keep the scary dreams away,
You **must** make time for rest and play.

Remember nightmares are not real,
No matter how they make you feel.

Dreams are movies in your mind;
Choose to leave them all behind.

Or change the end to something new...
Rewrite the script, it's up to you!
Aww!
Oops!

Too many "what if's," all unknown,
the choice to make is yours alone.
Don't dwell on things you can't control;
For that's when worry takes its toll!

what others think
how others act
my efforts
how I treat others and myself
how I react to my thoughts and feelings
the past
the weather
THINGS I CAN CONTROL
Focus on these!
THINGS I CANNOT CONTROL

But if you focus on the NOW,
You'll ask yourself the WHY and HOW.
And if you do what must be done,
Despite your worry you have won!

Why am I feeling
this way?
How can I help
myself feel
better?

Just take a step, and then two more...
You'll be much stronger than before.
Accept that you will make mistakes;
It's how you learn, that's what it takes!

I can choose to
do things even if
I feel worried or
afraid. If I fall,
I'll get back up!

The next time worry visits you,
You'll know exactly what to do.

You'll act despite the things you feel,
And work to make your wishes real!

Your worries must not stay for long;
Your heart is not where they belong.

With each step forward you will grow;
You're SO much stronger than you know!

Want freebies?

Get FREE emotional regulation activity sheets through our mailing list. Use your smartphone camera to scan the code below, then tap the link. Or visit our website!

@kimt.s.books - @kimtsbooks - kimtsbooks@gmail.com

www.kimtsbooks.com